Contents

1

Acknowledgements
The author wishes to thank Taro Shindo 3rd Dan, Richard Herd 3rd kyu and Catherine Shaw 6th kyu for demonstrating the techniques. The publishers would like to thank Rucanor for their photographic contribution to this book.

Rucanor

Photograph on page 45 courtesy of Sylvio Dokov. All other photographs by Martin Sellars.

Note Throughout the book karateka are referred to individually as 'he'. This should, of course, be taken to mean 'he or she' where appropriate.

Introduction

Karate is a Japanese fighting system which uses the hands and feet to deliver powerful punches, strikes and kicks. Karate is also both an exhilarating combat sport and a form of mental training. The word **karate** means 'empty hand' and the person who practises karate is known as a **karateka**.

Classical karate developed within an Eastern culture in which the main object in training was not so much to be able to defeat the opponent as to be able to defeat one's own fear and anger. A mind 'empty' of emotions was thought to be the best way of directing the 'hand' of karate, and the method by which this was achieved is known as **karate-do**, or 'the way of karate'.

Unfortunately, this understanding of karate's method has largely been lost now and 'empty hand' is generally thought to mean simply that no weapons are used.

Karate as we practise it today is relatively modern. But like most Oriental fighting systems, it is based on much older forms of combat, principally those from the southern Shaolin boxing schools of mainland China.

The immediate ancestor of modern karate is **to-te**, sometimes called **Okinawa te**. To-te was developed on Okinawa, the largest of the Ryukyu chain of islands which form a natural bridge between Japan and China. Okinawa's geographical position and foreign policies attracted Chinese soldiers and military attachés, who contributed both techniques and method to Okinawan martial practice.

Okinawan students often visited the Chinese mainland to further their martial art studies, bringing back new techniques and methods to throw into the melting pot which eventually became known either as **karate** ('China hand') or **Ryukyu kempo** ('Ryukyu boxing').

Just as there were many schools of Chinese martial art, so there were many Okinawan parallels. At first the schools were banned by Okinawa's Japanese overlords, so the students had to practise secretly. However, towards the end of the nineteenth century, the Japanese prohibitions were relaxed and karate appeared publicly.

To accommodate growing anti-Chinese feelings, the Japanese character (but not the pronunciation) for karate was changed from 'China hand' to 'empty hand'.

The schools of karate

There are four major schools or styles (**ryu**) of karate. They are:

- the **Shotokan**, founded by Gichin Funakoshi
- the **Goju ryu**, founded by Chojun Miyagi
- the **Shito ryu**, founded by Kenwa Mabuni
- the **Wado ryu**, founded by Hironori Ohtsuka.

There isn't an enormous difference between these four schools, and most techniques are common to all. There are differences, however, in the way they are practised, so it is not a good idea to mix the styles early in your training.

There is no 'best' style of karate, and you should beware of clubs which tell you there is. Having said that, each style has certain characteristics which may suit some individuals more than others.

The following are some general characteristics of the major styles. But be warned, though, that not all styles are well represented throughout Britain, and you may have to settle for an alternative to your first choice.

Shotokan

Shotokan means 'Shoto's club', where **Shoto** was the pen-name of the founder. This style was developed by an Okinawan teacher named Gichin Funakoshi. Worldwide, it is probably the most popular.

The style uses low, strong stances with emphasis placed on generating maximum power. Importance is attached to what is called **kime** or 'focus': this is the point in any technique where maximum physical and mental power is developed. During focus, all of the muscles of the body tense to make it as strong and as rigid as possible.

Competition is not over-emphasised, but when practised it is tough and uncompromising, scoring only those techniques which, if uncontrolled, could be expected to injure the opponent severely.

Goju ryu

Goju ryu means 'hard/soft school' because it combines the elements of yielding and great strength in one system. It was originated by the Okinawan Chojun Miyagi.

The style is very traditional, and competition plays only a minor part. Goju ryu uses many circular movements, and its stances are higher than those found in Shotokan. Unusually, Goju ryu incorporates a fitness training programme designed to increase strength, endurance and speed. Goju ryu also makes use of the punching post, or **makiwara**, to develop the correct fist profile.

At the core of the style is the stance known as **sanchin**. This is a very strong platform for resisting or responding to attacks. The centre of gravity is kept low, and all power is developed from the hips – the upper body is less important.

Shito ryu

The name of this school is taken from the names of the founder's two teachers. Shito ryu was originated by an Okinawan policeman called Kenwa Mabuni.

In this one style are found the principal characteristics of both of the previous styles. On the whole, the movements tend to be shorter and crisper than Shotokan, and lighter and faster than those of Goju ryu. Its techniques incorporate an economy of movement and grace not seen in any of the other styles.

Competition plays a large part in this style.

Wado ryu

Unlike the preceding styles, Hironori Ohtsuka's **Wado ryu** ('way of peace school') is firmly Japanese-based. Ohtsuka was Funakoshi's senior student and a noted Japanese martial artist in his own right. It was therefore inevitable that he would incorporate elements of his martial knowledge into karate. This he did to great effect, producing a graceful, fast style which relied rather more than other schools on sophisticated evasion movements.

The style avoids direct confrontation of force against force, and the techniques are typically fast and performed with a snapping action. Like those in Shito ryu, Wado ryu students are successful in open competitions. Indeed, it was Ohtsuka who pioneered karate competition.

Other styles

The following styles are also practised in Britain:

- **Shukokai** ('way for all'), or more correctly, **Tani ha Shito ryu**, was founded by Chojiro Tani, a former senior Japanese student of the Shito ryu founder, Kenwa Mabuni. Shukokai emphasises the generation of maximum power in punches and kicks, using a theory of power generation that is both very interesting and convincing.
- **Shotokai** ('Shoto's way') separated from the Shotokan after Funakoshi's death. The Shotokai felt that karate was moving too far from its original form and wanted to return to more traditional ways. Training is similar to Shotokan, though there is less emphasis on focus. There is no competition, and only high grades are allowed to free spar.

• **Kyokushinkai** ('the way of ultimate truth') was founded by Masutatsu Oyama, a Korean student of Funakoshi. Oyama disagreed with the linear way in which Shotokan was practised, and he incorporated circular techniques into his style. Kyokushinkai favours a particularly strenuous and potentially hazardous form of competition known as 'knockdown'.

Safety

Karate can be a strenuous activity. Check whether you're fit enough to practise. This is particularly important for novices over the age of 40.

Don't train soon after eating a large meal. This is because the process of digestion uses up a considerable amount of blood which is otherwise required by the exercising muscles – including the heart – and cramp may result.

Make sure that the club instructor knows if you suffer from any complaint likely to affect your ability to train. If the instructor is aware of your health condition, he can check your performance and he may spot the onset of symptoms before you do.

Certain types of virus infections can have serious side effects on heart muscle, so avoid sharp bangs on the chest, and sudden training spurts, if you have a cold.

Choosing your club

Choosing the correct karate club is the most important step you will take in your karate career. Pick the wrong one and you could waste many years of hard practice, because not all karate clubs are good clubs. Unfortunately, there is no legal requirement for karate instructors to be recognised by a competent national body, and few black belts are properly trained coaches.

Most karate clubs are run by the instructor; only a few are run by a committee of the membership, and others are limited companies. The club you choose ought to be a member of an association, and the association itself should be a direct or indirect member of a national karate governing body.

Go to your local leisure centre and look at the notice board. Note the training nights and times from the posters you see there but avoid clubs which employ hype, such as 'best', 'biggest', 'strongest', etc. These claims are nearly always false.

Visit the club on its training nights, though you may find that some clubs will not allow you to watch training. Cross these clubs from your list!

Is the instructor a black belt? Is he clean and well presented? Does he treat the students with courtesy? Look at the number of coloured belts practising. If the club has been running for about a couple of years, there should be some brown or black belts present. This shows that students have remained with the instructor, an indication that the instructor is a good one.

Ask the instructor whether he is a member of an association, and whether that association is affiliated to a national governing body. If the answer to both of these questions is 'Yes', and if you like the atmosphere in the club, then consider joining.

What will it cost?

When you join a karate club you will pay an annual fee which registers you as a member. This currently varies between £5 and £25 per year. In many cases, the fee also includes an individual registration with an association or a governing body. Typically, this latter registration includes a valuable personal accident and third party indemnity insurance. Ask the instructor for full details. (*Note* All prices quoted in the text are accurate at the time of writing.)

You will be issued automatically with a membership receipt within 31 days of joining. This comes in a 'licence' book which serves to record your personal progress within the association. Don't worry about insurance during those first 31 days, because if you paid your fee immediately on joining, the instructor will have notified the association HQ and you will be indemnified.

Whatever you do, make sure you pay your fee immediately on joining because accidents tend to happen more frequently in the early days of training, i.e. that is when you need your insurance most.

Each time you train you may be required to pay a 'mat fee'. This varies from a few pence to a couple of pounds.

The average length of a session is 90 minutes, and it is usual to train at least twice a week.

Clothing

There is no need to buy a training uniform immediately – a T-shirt and a pair of training bottoms will be fine. At some stage, however, you will want to buy a karate suit, or **karategi**. Try to put off buying one for as long as possible because you may find karate is not, after all, to your liking, and a second-hand karate suit is difficult to re-sell at a reasonable price.

Most clubs can supply you with a karategi cheaper than the price you would pay if you went to a normal sports shop. Alternatively, you can write to a specialist martial arts shop, getting the name and address from a martial arts magazine.

There are usually three qualities of suit offered. The cheapest is a light weight suit at around £18; then there is a medium weight suit costing about £30; finally, a heavy weight tournament suit can cost over £100. If you can afford it, buy the medium weight: it will last longer and look better.

Always buy your suit a size too large because, regardless of what the manufacturer claims, suits shrink every time they are washed. Make sure your new suit has a good deal of room in the thigh and groin areas because you must be able to lift your knee up high without the material pulling.

Karate suits are supplied with a white belt, so check with the instructor that this is the correct colour to start from.

Keep your suit clean with regular washing at 40°C. A tidy appearance shows the correct attitude to training, whereas a dirty or ripped suit indicates a bad attitude. Buy a pair of flip-flop sandals to keep your feet clean as you walk between the changing rooms and the training hall, and ask the instructor about buying fist mitts, shin guards and groin protectors. You will need these when you begin sparring practice.

Grading

You will be eligible to take a grading examination approximately every 48 hours of training. Grading examinations measure your progress and indicate the levels of skill attained by means of coloured belts. Although the number of grades and belt colours varies from school to school, the following is a common scheme:

- red or white belt
- white belt
- yellow belt
- orange belt
- green belt
- purple belt
- brown belt (three grades)
- black belt.

The fee for a grading examination varies tremendously and it is sometimes charged according to the grade being examined. A typical fee might be £10 for coloured belts, £30 for the first black belt.

A new belt costs around £3 and can be bought through the club, from a sports shop or from a specialist supplier. Judo belts are quite acceptable. But don't be tempted to dye your old belt the new colour because the sweat of training always causes the dye to run and colour your karate suit.

There is a right and a wrong way to tie a belt. Start by wrapping it twice around your waist, and draw the ends to an equal length. Tuck one end up the inside of both coils, and bring it over the top. Then bring the second end across and tuck the first under and through, pulling the knot tight. If you have succeeded, the belt ends will be of equal length and protruding from either side of the knot in the 'quarter-to-three' position.

Etiquette

Respect for the instructor and for class-mates is a cornerstone of good karate practice. Even the place of karate training, or **dojo** as it is known, is treated with respect. If nobody is in the dojo as you enter, pause at the entrance and face the centre of the room. Put your heels together and your hands flat against the front of your thighs. This posture is known as **attention stance**. Then perform a standing bow. If other people are in the dojo, then bow towards the senior grade.

Don't bow too far, just incline your upper body forwards. Make the bow smooth, and hesitate at the lowest point for a count of two before straightening up again. As befits the follower of any true fighting art, you should always be on the lookout for attack, so never look down at the floor as you bow.

Once you make the bow, you can step into the training hall.

Bow also when leaving the hall, even if you're leaving only for a short interval.

If you arrive after the class has started, don't just walk in. Bow towards the instructor and then exercise to warm up. If required, perform two kneeling bows as described later. Then stand or kneel conspicuously at the edge of the mat and wait to be called on by the class senior.

You will need to learn some of the terms you may come across in the dojo. The club instructor is correctly addressed as **sensei**, and any student senior to yourself as **sempai**. Students of lower grade are referred to as **kohei**.

Behaviour in the dojo identifies the true karateka, so don't talk noisily or act sloppily. If you sit down, then cross your legs so nobody will trip over them. It is the height of bad manners to smoke, or sprawl out on the floor. When standing, don't lounge against walls.

At the beginning of the training session you will be called to order. The class lines up and before taking your place, make sure the person in front of you has the same colour belt as you have. Tidy your karate suit, and check that your belt is fastened properly. Adopt attention stance and wait quietly.

When the class is settled, the senior will call **'Seiza!'** ('Kneel!'). Drop on to your right knee, keeping your hands to your sides, then bring your left knee down, alongside the first. Point your toes, and sit back on to your calves. Keep your back straight and hold your head up.

This position can be painful at first, especially for older students, so practise it at home on a carpet or cushion until you grow accustomed to it.

On the command **'Sensei ni rei!'**, the class bows to the teacher. Slide both palms forwards and incline your upper body into a low bow, making sure you can still see the person in front. Pause for two seconds at the lowest point before returning to an upright position. When the senior calls **'Otagai ni rei!'**, perform a second kneeling bow to your class-mates.

When the senior calls 'Kiritsu!', lift your left knee, then your right, and straighten into a standing attention stance once more.

This formal ritual is repeated at the end of the training session.

If your belt becomes unfastened at any time during training, drop on to one knee and re-tie it. If others are moving up behind you in class lines, use your common sense and step out of the line to avoid getting stepped on or tripped over.

When the instructor is showing the class a technique, make sure you can see the demonstration clearly. If you are chosen to assist the instructor, don't make fatuous remarks or move without being told. When training with a partner, avoid loud discussion and speak only when there is a need to. Even then, keep it short.

Remember, karate training begins and ends with courtesy.

Warming up

People of all shapes and sizes can practise karate. Having said that, karate practice means training your body in ways it is not used to. If you begin training immediately, this may cause aches and pains, or even injuries. It is far better to introduce your body gradually to the rigours of training by means of the warm-up. The warm-up progressively increases your heart rate so that more blood is pumped to working muscles. It also works your limbs and body in a way appropriate for the training that is to follow.

Exercises

● Run on the spot, raising your knees high and pumping your arms. Begin slowly, then gradually increase speed. Run for around one minute. If you prefer you can substitute skipping for running. Then jump on the spot, making every tenth jump higher than the rest, while pulling your knees to your chest. Spin around quarter, half and full turns as you jump, but be careful not to over-tire yourself before training begins.

● Recover your breath with a gentle leg stretching exercise. Spread your legs apart and lower your weight slowly and asymetrically on to the left foot. Keep the soles of both feet pressed to the floor. Support your weight by resting your palms on your knees. Hold the lowest position for a count of five. Then smoothly shift your weight across so it comes to lie over the other foot. Repeat the exercise at least five times on each side.

● Next, extend the stretch by sinking down on one leg while fully extending the other. Drop your bottom down as low as you can get it, and hold this lowest position for a count of five. Keeping the body low, swing across so your weight comes to lie over the other foot. Repeat this exercise five times on each side.

● Sit down and use your hands to work the ankles through their full range of movement.

● Stand up and lean forwards, placing the palms of your hands flat on the floor. Keep your knees straight. Then walk forwards on your hands and lower your thighs to the mat. Pause and then walk backwards into the bent-over standing position once more. Straighten up and repeat the exercise four more times.

● Step forwards with your left foot and place your hands on your hips. Lean back as far as you can, hold this position for five seconds and then straighten up. Return to the standing position and then step forwards with your right foot. Repeat the exercise five times on each side.

● Sit down and splay your feet out wide, keeping the backs of your knees pressed firmly to the mat. Reach forwards with your hands and skim them over the surface of the mat without touching it. Swing your trunk from side to side as you reach towards each ankle in turn.

● Lie on your back with the knees bent, the soles of the feet pressing against the mat, and the hands folded behind your neck. Curl your upper body forwards so the shoulder blades leave the mat. Try to touch your knees with your elbows. Repeat the exercise ten to 20 times. Vary its effect by twisting your body as you sit up, alternately touching each knee with the opposite elbow.

● Stand up and extend your arms above your head. Turn the hands back-to-back and link the fingers. Lean as far as you can to the left, then to the right. Keep pushing up with your hands as you stretch, and repeat the exercise five times on each side.

● Stand with the feet shoulder-width apart. Lean forwards and let your fingers touch the mat. Rotate your trunk in a wide circle, turning first one way then the other, and keeping your hands extended the whole time. Repeat five times each way.

● Drop on to your front and place your palms shoulder-width apart on the mat. Look forwards and straighten your elbows fully, thrusting your body clear. Then lower yourself down until your chest brushes the mat. If you can't manage any press-ups at all, drop your knees to the mat and try again. Do at least ten press-ups, gradually improving over the weeks until you can manage 50 at any one session.

● Stand up and circle your arms, so that each arm travels in the opposite direction.

● Work your wrist joints through their full range of movement.

● Turn your head from side to side. Do this smoothly and don't force your head to turn too far. Tilt your head back and then drop it forwards, so that the chin brushes your chest. Lean your head sideways on to one shoulder, then on to the other.

This is a thorough warm-up, and you should be ready now for training. Finish off the warm-up by doing the first few manoeuvres of each karate technique slowly, and gradually increase power as your limbs begin to feel freer.

Cooling down

At the end of the training session your muscles will be full of fatigue-producing lactic acid. This must be pumped out or it will remain to cause aches and pains the next day. Cool down by practising techniques at a gradually diminishing speed after training finishes. Then do some gentle stretching exercises based on those used in the warm-up.

Making a fist

Below the roots of your fingers, at the top of your palm, is a ridge formed by the underside of the knuckles. Fold your fingers down so that their tips contact it (*see* fig. 1), then close the fist fully and lock the fingers in by folding your thumb across the index and middle fingers (fig. 2). If the fist is made correctly, a right angle will be formed by the fingers and the back of the hand. This is difficult to achieve at first, but you must keep working at it because a wrongly-formed fist may damage the skin of the knuckles. Don't let your thumb poke forwards or it will catch in someone's sleeve, and do not enclose it by the fingers or it will be damaged when your fist strikes something hard. Most of the time your fist can be relaxed slightly, but always tighten it fully on impact.

Because the knuckles of your fist do not all lie in one line, you will be able to land only *some* of them on the target at any one time. Karate uses the index and middle knuckles, so aim your fist so that these alone make contact. The middle knuckle protrudes further than the others, so take extra care to avoid landing on it alone. Keep your forearm in line with the back of your fist to stop the wrist from folding on impact (fig. 2).

▲ *Fig. 1 Making a fist (1)*

▲ *Fig. 2 Making a fist (2)*

11

The basic punch

The basic punch is practised from a feet-apart stance known as **ready stance** (**fudodachi**). Begin from attention stance by stepping to the side with the left foot, then with the right, until both are approximately shoulder-width apart. The feet are turned slightly outwards and the closed fists are carried in front of the thighs.

Extend your right fist and twist it so that the palm turns downwards, but don't let your shoulder lift or move forwards behind the action. Bring your extended fist into the mid-line of the body. Now open your left hand and bring your forearm across the chest, just below the extended right arm. Draw back your fist to the hip, rotating it palm-upwards as it comes to rest. Move at exactly the same speed with your left hand, extending it and turning the palm forwards (fig. 3).

On the command, sharply withdraw your left hand and close it into a fist. Simultaneously thrust out the right hand, so that the two fists pass each

▲ *Fig. 3 The basic punch (1)*

12

▲ *Fig. 4 The basic punch (2)*

▲ *Fig. 5 The basic punch (3)*

other at the mid-way point (fig. 4). As the right elbow extends, so the left elbow flexes. In the last few instants, both fists suddenly rotate so that the right turns palm-down, and the left turns palm-upwards (fig. 5). This action *must* be simultaneous. Keep both fists relaxed until now, then clench them tightly as imaginary impact occurs. Relax your shoulders and draw back your right fist while extending your open left hand once more.

Be prepared to repeat the punch up to ten times on one side, then change your arms over and practise punching with the left fist.

Examine the way you are punching to see whether there is any way to make the punch stronger without leaning your shoulders into the action. Take your hip back slightly as you withdraw a fist, and then twist it forwards a few degrees as that same fist extends. Do not exaggerate this movement. Then do the same with your shoulders but, again, do not move them more than a couple of degrees. Also, allow the shoulders to drop slightly as the punching arm reaches full extension because this locks the arm and gives it extra rigidity.

All the punches you will learn subsequently are based on this combination of pull-back with punching action. Unfortunately, most beginners concentrate only on the punch. This produces incorrect technique which, if it isn't rectified at an early stage, is more difficult to eradicate later.

13

Generating powerful impacts

Each of us is limited in the degree of impact we can generate with our punches and kicks. The object of power training is to raise impact force to the maximum that we can achieve realistically.

In generating power, techniques must be delivered as quickly as possible. Furthermore, it is vital that on impact the fist is still accelerating – though as near to maximum speed as possible – so make sure your range is accurate.

Always begin with a relaxed action, throwing the fist into the target and then tightening up just as you are about to land.

Regardless of the technique used, always try to put body weight behind it. A forward shift of body weight over even a couple of centimetres is sufficient to produce a substantial bonus in impact energy. This energy is also invaluable for soaking up the recoil produced by a blow, and this is particularly important if you are a small person striking a larger opponent.

Try to develop power from the hips. By letting the hip twist first, the spine is tensioned. When that tension is released it moves the upper body with it, driving the shoulder forwards behind the blow.

Whether delivering a punch, kick or strike, it always makes sense to withdraw the hand or foot promptly afterwards, so that it cannot be seized by the opponent.

Kiai

The term **kiai** is not easy to translate directly, but it indicates a harmony between your will to strike the target and the energy you put into the technique. At the conclusion of any powerful technique, the karateka injects every ounce of power and determination, locking up all the muscles for an instant of time. As the diaphragm (the muscular band below the ribs, responsible for breathing) tightens, air is driven out and gives rise to the kiai.

The sound kiai makes is formed into a short, explosive, monosyllabic 'EEE!', which is in many ways similar to the grunt or gasp made when pushing a car, or lifting a heavy object.

Kiai occurs during the performance of any intense action or technique.

Punching on the move

Having practised the basic punch, the next thing to try is punching on the move. There are two techniques in this section – lunge punch and reverse punch. Both begin from **forward stance**, or **zenkutsu dachi**. The class will perform them usually in lines, advancing until space is used up, then turning on command to advance in the opposite direction.

Forward stance

From ready stance, take a long step back with your right foot. As you are stepping, extend your right fist palm-downwards and bring the left fist thumb-upwards to the top of your right shoulder (fig. 6). Then draw back your right fist to the hip, and twist it palm-upwards. At the same time, thrust downwards with your left arm so that it sweeps across the body and comes to lie just above and to the outside of your

▲ Fig. 6 Forward stance (1)

▲ Fig. 7 Forward stance (2)

15

leading knee. Turn your left fist palm-downwards as movement comes to a stop, and pull your hips back 45° from forward-facing (fig. 7).

Your body weight is concentrated 65% over the bent leading knee, which comes to lie immediately above the instep. Your right knee is fully extended with the sole planted firmly on the mat. Your leading foot points straight ahead and the trailing foot is turned outwards by no more than 45°.

The height of forward stance varies from style to style, though the width is always such that the outer edges of the feet are vertically below the shoulders. Too much side-step and your groin is open to attack; too little and the stance is unstable. If the front knee is not bent sufficiently, the leading foot does not bear down and stability is lost. If the leading knee falls inwards, the stance is weakened. If the rear heel is off the floor or the knee is bent, the stance's ability to absorb recoil is reduced.

Lunge punch

Lunge punch is known either as **oi zuki**, or as **junzuki**. The height of delivery

▲ *Fig. 8 Lunge punch (1)*

▲ *Fig. 9 Lunge punch (2)*

16

varies according to the instructions given, such that **jodan** punches are aimed towards the face, **chudan** towards the mid section, and **gedan** towards the lower stomach and groin.

Start from left forward stance. Skim the right foot forwards, so that it passes close by the left. The left foot turns outwards slightly as this happens. Keep your height constant throughout, and don't let your left arm waggle about (fig. 8). Continue forwards with your right foot and as weight begins to settle on to it, pull back your left fist sharply and punch with the right (fig. 9). Rotate both fists simultaneously at the end of their motion.

The timing of the punch is critical. To gain from the momentum generated, the punch must land on the target while the body is still moving. But if started too early, it will pull you forwards and off balance. Begin your punch even as your weight begins to settle on the front foot.

Getting the step right is difficult, and novices usually find their stance widening or narrowing, or drawing out or shortening as they progress.

Turn into head block

Head block (jodan uke) uses a diagonal upwards and outwards rolling action of the forearm to deflect the opponent's face punch.

Assume you are in right forward stance when you run out of space and have to turn around. On the command '**Mawatte jodan uke!**', first look over your left shoulder to check whether it is safe to turn. Then step across with your left foot, keeping the knee bent and your heel clear of the floor (fig. 10). Twist your hips in an anti-clockwise direction, and bend your right elbow so that the forearm protects your face (fig. 11). Pull back the right fist as you thrust the left diagonally across the front of your chest and face (fig. 12).

As the block engages the opponent's punch, so the forearm rotates until the little finger side of the fist faces upwards. This forearm rotation is important because it strengthens the block and improves the degree of deflection achieved. Bring the crook in the blocking elbow close to the side of your head and you will resist more easily attempts to smash the forearm down.

▲ *Fig. 10 Turn into head block (1)*

17

▲ *Fig. 11 Turn into head block (2)*

▲ *Fig. 12 Turn into head block (3)*

The block intercepts the punch before it reaches the face, and bumps it upwards so that it clears the head. Perform a strong kiai as you block the opponent's punch.

Practise the turn and block several times, turning each way alternately.

Reverse punch

Practise **reverse punch (gyakuzuki)** from forward stance by first punching without stepping forwards (fig. 13). This ensures that your correct arm is leading. Note how the punching hip moves forwards until the hips face completely to the front. This revised hip position draws the leading foot back and outwards, while rotating it slightly inwards.

Push outwards on the leading knee to prevent it sagging inwards.

To practise advancing reverse punch, first turn the leading foot outwards, then transfer your weight in the usual manner but as you bring your rear foot forwards, also curve it inwards so that it slides past the front leg (fig. 14). Then allow it to curve out by the same distance and angle. As you complete the

▲ *Fig. 13 Reverse punch (1)*

▲ *Fig. 14 Reverse punch (2)*

▲ *Fig. 15 Reverse punch (3)*

19

step, draw back your leading fist and punch with the reverse hand. Rotate both feet so that they are parallel or slightly converging (fig. 15).

Hold your leading arm well forwards as you step, and don't wave it about or swing your shoulders. Time the punching action as for the lunge punch.

The purpose of the semi-circular step is to open your hips out and 'cock' the punch. The hips move from front-facing to 45°, turned away as the new lead foot takes up its final position. Then as weight moves forwards on to the leading leg, so the hips swing forwards again and the punch is thrust out. Firmly clench both fists, and simultaneously tighten and rotate them as they come to rest.

Turn and lower parry

Lower parry (gedan barai) is used against a variety of straight attacks aimed at the chest or stomach. Use the little finger side of your forearm in a diagonal thrusting and wiping action across the front of the body, so that it comes to rest above and to the outside of the leading knee. Use this block with caution, and ensure that it sweeps attacking techniques to the side rather than meeting them full-on.

Assume you are in right reverse punch stance, with your left fist leading when you run out of space. First glance over your left shoulder to ensure the coast is clear, then slide your left foot straight across while keeping both knees bent and the left heel clear of the floor. As you are turning, flex your left elbow so that the little finger of your left fist rests lightly against your right shoulder (fig. 16). Then twist your hips counter-clockwise while sweeping and thrusting downwards with your left fist (*see* fig. 7 again).

Turning into the lower parry, you will take up forward stance automatically, leading with the left foot and left fist, and with your right hip withdrawn 45° from forward-facing. But when you punch without stepping forwards, your stance changes and the right hip turns fully forward-facing.

▲ *Fig. 16 Turn and lower parry*

20

Striking techniques

Striking techniques use the hands in different ways to the punches we have so far considered. Practise striking techniques from fighting stance.

Fighting stance

Fighting stance (**jiu dachi**) is used extensively in sparring; hence its name.

Begin from ready stance by stepping backwards with your right foot until your body weight is distributed 50/50 over both feet. Ensure that your stance has side-step, i.e. the heels must not be in one line. Side-step provides side-to-side balance. Turn your leading foot slightly inwards, and rotate the back foot so that it faces towards the front. Bend both knees equally, and turn the hips 45° from forward-facing.

Your left fist moves forwards into the projected centre line of your body, and the elbow flexes until the fist is at shoulder height. The right fist takes up a palm-upwards guard position just above the knot in your belt (fig. 17).

▲ *Fig. 17 Fighting stance*

Fighting stance must not be so long as to slow forward and backward movement, but neither must it be so short that you are easily driven backwards by a determined attacker.

Back fist

Back fist (**uraken**) uses the back of the knuckles in a circular strike to the temple, the bridge of the nose, or the jaw. Like all circular techniques, it is difficult to block.

The punching elbow is nearest to the target and this lifts until it points directly where you want the fist to go (fig. 18). The hips then rotate away from the opponent as the striking arm 'unrolls' into the target. Lash out with the fist, striking with the back of the two large knuckles (fig. 19).

Lean into the strike and relax your elbow and wrist until just before impact, then tense them. Allow natural joint elasticity to snap the wrist back.

By turning the body *away* from the strike delivery, the shoulders open out and the full length of the arm can be used to advantage.

▲ *Fig. 18 Back fist (1)*

▲ *Fig. 19 Back fist (2)*

▲ *Fig. 20 Hammer fist (1)*

▲ *Fig. 21 Hammer fist (2)*

Hammer fist

Hammer fist (tettsui) uses the closed fist in a clubbing action.

Take up left fighting stance, and seize the opponent's leading arm with your left hand. Draw his upper body diagonally forwards and down. At the same time, raise your right fist behind your head (fig. 20). Strike downwards as the opponent's head comes into range, landing the strike with the pad of flesh between the base of the little finger and the wrist. Clench your fist tightly on impact (fig. 21). Inject extra power by bending your knees slightly and by sinking your hips as the strike is about to land.

23

▲ *Fig. 22 Knife hand (1)*

▲ *Fig. 23 Knife hand (2)*

Knife hand

Knife hand (shuto) uses the little finger edge of the palm to concentrate a great deal of force over a small area. Strike with the area that lies between the base of your little finger and the wrist. Stiffen your fingers on impact to prevent them from jarring together painfully. Cup the hand slightly during horizontal circular strikes.

Stand in right fighting stance, facing the opponent. He reaches for your lapel with his left hand but you evade this by stepping to the right with your leading foot and twisting your hips towards him. Draw your right hand to your right ear, as though saluting. At the same time, take his leading elbow in your left hand and draw his upper body forwards and down (fig. 22).

Twist your right hip forwards and chop at the side of the opponent's neck, turning your hand palm-upwards as it makes contact (fig. 23).

Palm heel

Palm heel (**shotei**) uses the palm of the hand as though it were a fist. Bend your fingers so that the tips brush the pad of flesh running along the top of the palm, and fold the thumb in. Flex your wrist back as far as it will go.

Throw the hand forwards with the fingers and thumb relaxed, then as soon as the strike is about to make contact the hand tightens, the elbow straightens, and the palm heel slams home (fig. 24).

Elbow strikes

Elbow (**empi**) is an effective and versatile short range weapon. Impact is made with the tip of the elbow rather than with the forearm, since the former is more effective at concentrating force.

Face the opponent in right fighting stance. Take his leading guard hand across his body, so he is prevented from counter-attacking you. Slide your trailing foot forwards slightly, and swing your right elbow up and around so that it clips the side of the opponent's jaw (fig. 25). Generate maximum impact by striking as you shift body weight forwards, and by turning your hips 'through' the opponent.

◀ *Fig. 24 Palm heel*

25

▲ *Fig. 25 Elbow strike*

Kicking techniques

Front kick

Front kick (**maegeri**) uses the thick pad of flesh that runs beneath the toes. Point your foot in a straight line with your shin, and pull your toes back. It is sometimes difficult to do this correctly, so practise by placing the sole of your foot flat on the floor, then raising the heel as high as you can.

Begin from left fighting stance by first changing your guard and twisting your supporting leg outwards. As this happens (i.e. not afterwards) raise your right foot, lifting the sole directly from the floor. Don't lift the heel first or you will find it difficult to get your foot into the correct configuration. Bring your knee up until it is pointing at the opponent's face (fig. 26).

As your knee reaches the correct height, begin thrusting your lower leg out so that the sole of your foot travels horizontally into the target, with toes pulled back (fig. 27). After delivering the kick, pull your foot back and set it down

▲ *Fig. 26 Front kick (1)*

▲ *Fig. 27 Front kick (2)*

gently in a forward position. Novices seldom lift the kicking knee high enough, so the foot moves in an upward arc which skates up the front of the target, instead of penetrating it. The cor-rect kicking action requires the knee to drop as the foot thrusts out.

Keep your elbows to your side so that they don't flap about, and don't straighten your supporting leg. Take care not to move your body weight too far forwards or your spent kick will simply slap down, in easy reach of the opponent.

27

One-step front kick

One-step front kick (surikomi-maegeri) uses a scissors step, both to cover distance and to accelerate the technique. Begin from left fighting stance and skim your right foot forwards while turning it outwards (fig. 28). Then perform front kick.

Your guard remains unchanged as you step, and you can vary the distance to be covered by the length of the scissors step.

Accelerate smoothly through the step, and perform the kick so it is part of the movement. Then set the spent kick down carefully.

◀ *Fig. 28 One-step front kick*

Roundhouse kick

Roundhouse kick (mawashigeri) is one of the most popular kicking techniques in karate. The instep is used in this version, that being the upper part of the foot between the base of the toes and the front of the ankle. Kick safely with the instep by straightening your ankle fully and turning your toes down. Kick from the correct range and angle, or you may hurt your foot.

From left fighting stance, rotate your shoulders strongly to the left and lift the right foot off the mat. Your hips then follow the shoulders, so that the supporting foot swivels anti-clockwise through 120°. The flexed right knee is brought across the front of the body (fig. 29), where it can act as a guard against the opponent's sudden counter-attack.

If you rotate your hips sufficiently, then the right will roll over the top of the left. Begin straightening your lower leg as the knee turns towards the target. Strike the target with your instep (fig. 30), and withdraw the spent kick sharply. Set the foot down gently into a new fighting stance.

▲ *Fig. 29 Roundhouse kick (1)*

▲ *Fig. 30 Roundhouse kick (2)*

Always lean away from the rising kick so as not to inhibit hip action. Relax your shoulders so that they don't hunch up, and maintain your guard throughout.

Novices seldom have sufficient hip flexibility to raise the knee high enough.

Work on your flexibility while kicking at a height you can manage – even if this is quite low. It is important that you learn the feel of a correct kick, so don't be tempted to kick higher than your flexibility allows: this will cause unwelcome technique adaptations.

Incidentally, you can perform roundhouse kick also with the ball of the foot. Apart from having to change your foot configuration, the kick is scarcely different.

Side kick

Side kick (**yokogeri**) uses the heel and little toe edge of the foot in a direct, thrusting attack to the opponent's knee or mid section. Practise the correct foot shape by lifting your big toe while depressing the others. Like roundhouse kick, side kick requires a good deal of hip flexibility because the knee must be lifted until the heel is at the same height as the intended target.

The kick is best practised from a **straddle stance** (**shiko dachi**). This resembles the position taken by a rider on horseback. Height of stance varies from style to style but configuration is the same, with the body upright and the weight distributed evenly.

Begin from ready stance and step to the side, first with the left foot, then with the right. Let your feet rotate outwards slightly but make sure your knees are directly above your ankles (fig. 31). Keep your back straight and don't let your bottom poke out. Hold your fists relaxed at the thighs.

Lean to the left and raise your right knee. Twist slightly on your supporting foot, and point the heel of your right foot

▲ *Fig. 31 Side kick (1)*

30

▲ *Fig. 32 Side kick (2)*

▲ *Fig. 33 Side kick (3)*

directly towards the target (fig. 32). Simultaneously twist further on your supporting foot, and thrust your right heel directly into the target (fig. 33), remembering to lift the big toe while depressing the others.

Lean back to counter-balance the weight of your extending leg, and maintain an effective guard throughout. After kicking, pull your knee back against your chest before setting it down in straddle stance.

Back kick

Practise **back kick** (**ushirogeri**) from a **back stance** (**kokutsu-dachi**). Begin from left fighting stance by drawing your weight back until 60% of it is over the rear foot. Your right knee is now strongly flexed, and the foot is vertically below your right hip. Turn your right foot until it is at 90° to the leading foot.

Your left foot reaches forwards and rests only lightly on the mat, with the heel raised. The hips are 45° away from forward-facing, and there is no side-step. Carry your guard as normal (fig. 34).

Perform back kick by sliding your front foot half a pace to the right and

▼ *Fig. 34 Back kick (1)*

▼ *Fig. 35 Back kick (2)*

turning your body clockwise until your back faces the opponent. Turn your head sharply round so that you lose sight of him for the shortest possible time (fig. 35). Your weight is now over the left foot. Lift your right foot and thrust it back in a straight line, heel-first into the target (fig. 36). Point the ball of the foot towards the floor. Drop the spent kick to the floor as though you were performing a turn (fig. 37), and turn into a new stance.

Turn your hips fully or the kick will be off centre. Back kick involves turning your back on the opponent, so only use it when it is safe to do so.

▼ *Fig. 36 Back kick (3)*

▼ *Fig. 37 Back kick (4)*

Blocking techniques

Blocking techniques use an arm or leg to prevent an attack from reaching you. Normally they are associated with an evasion movement that removes your body from the direct line of attack.

We have already practised head block and lower parry in conjunction with lunge and reverse punches. Now we will look at the two mid section forearm blocks. One uses the thumb side of your forearm (the 'inside'), the other uses the little finger side (the 'outside'), to sweep incoming techniques away from the target.

Inner forearm block

The Japanese name for this block is **chudan uchi-uke**.

Face your partner in left fighting stance. He faces you in left forward stance. Then he steps forwards and attempts to strike you in the chest with lunge punch. Even as he begins to

▲ *Fig. 38 Inner forearm block (1)*

move, step back with your left leg into forward stance and drop your right forearm palm-downwards across your stomach (fig. 38). Leave your left guard hand where it is. As you take up right forward stance withdraw your left guard hand strongly to the hip, and draw your left hip back until it faces 45° from straight ahead. Swing your right forearm upwards until the fist reaches the same level as your shoulders, and there is a 90° angle at the elbow. Sharp-

▲ *Fig. 39 Inner forearm block (2)*

▲ *Fig. 40 Inner forearm block (3)*

ly rotate your right forearm so that the palm turns back towards you.

If you have timed this correctly, your forearm will swing upwards across the path of the opponent's punch and deflect it across his body (fig. 39). Then turn your hips, pin the opponent's elbow with your right palm (fig. 40), and perform a strong reverse punch into his head. Remember to block *as* you are stepping back.

Training with a partner in this way is useful because in addition to teaching you how to block a real punch, it also introduces you to the concepts of timing and distance.

35

Outer forearm block

The Japanese name for this block is **chudan soto-uchi**. However, different schools sometimes reverse the names for the two forearm blocks, so check which is the appropriate name in your style.

Start as for the previous sequence except that this time your opponent begins from right forward stance. Then he steps forwards and attempts to strike you in the chest with left lunge punch. As he begins to move, step back with your left foot into right forward stance and bring your right fist to the side of your right ear (fig. 41). Leave your left guard hand in its original position.

As you settle into right forward stance, draw your left fist back and turn your hips 45° from forward-facing. Then swing your right forearm across your chest, flexing the elbow to 90° so that the fist is at the same level as your shoulders. Rotate your forearm as it makes contact with the opponent's fist so that the knuckles turn away from you.

Block *as* you step back, not once you have finished moving. If you have timed

▼ *Fig. 41 Outer forearm block (1)*

▼ *Fig. 42 Outer forearm block (2)*

things correctly, your forearm will sweep horizontally across the path of the opponent's punch, and deflect it (fig. 42).

Complete the sequence by shifting your weight forwards slightly and lunge-punching the opponent's head with your right fist (fig. 43). Provided that you shift body weight behind the punch, it becomes both effective and powerful. Then withdraw into left fighting stance.

Always bring your blocking elbow close to your ribs. The twisting of the forearm and the clenching of the fist near the end of the blocking action ensure a more efficient deflection.

Knife block

Knife block (**shuto-uke**) uses the little finger edge of the hand to deflect a punch or a strike. We have encountered this hand shape already when we practised the knife hand strike (*see* page 24).

Take up ready stance as the opponent faces you in right forward stance. The opponent steps forwards and attempts to punch you in the face. Even as he moves, step *diagonally* back and outwards with your right foot, and take up left back stance. As you move back, extend your right hand and turn the palm down to the floor. Bring your left hand around so that it almost cups your right ear (fig. 44), then pull your right hand back and turn it palm-upwards in front of your chest. At the same time, withdraw your right hip and shoulder,

▼ *Fig. 43 Outer forearm block (3)*

▲ *Fig. 44 Knife block (1)*

37

▲ *Fig. 45 Knife block (2)*

▲ *Fig. 46 Knife block (3)*

and cut outwards with your left hand so that the little finger edge leads (fig. 45). Trap the opponent's forearm with your left hand, and attack his floating ribs with knife hand (fig. 46). Pulling back the right hip. shoulder and arm (in that order) provides power for the block. Twisting your palm forwards also adds focus to the movement.

Scooping block

Scooping block (suki-uke) catches and lifts the opponent's front kick. It is performed together with a strong hip-twisting motion which takes the body out of harm's way.

Face the opponent in left fighting stance. Step outwards with your leading foot even as the opponent lifts his right foot to perform front kick. Twist your hips clockwise so that both feet pivot, then bring your left hand around and under the opponent's Achilles tendon to lift and deflect his front kick (fig. 47). Twist your hips back towards the opponent, and allow his spent front kick to fall away from you.

Quickly withdraw your left arm, and perform reverse punch with your right fist into the opponent's head or kidneys (fig. 48).

The most common fault is under-twisting the hips, so ensure that you turn sideways-on to the opponent. Another common mistake is a failure to twist back to forward-facing when performing the reverse punch.

Fig. 47 Scooping block (1) ▶

▲ *Fig. 48 Scooping block (2)*

Combination techniques

Basic techniques can be linked together into a series such that after the first technique is performed, the next in line is already prepared and ready to go. Whereas one technique can be blocked, a whole series of techniques aimed at different targets and from different angles puts the defender under pressure, and one may strike home.

When assembling techniques choose those which follow each other naturally. Then select a different target for each technique so that the defender is forced to use a bewildering variety of blocks to cope. Ensure the techniques follow each other as quickly as possible, and be able to perform them while advancing, retreating or evading.

Maintain balance and guard throughout the combination, and retrieve each technique properly after use. Make sure individual techniques are performed correctly before the next is used. Many novices gloss over the first technique, concentrating all their efforts on the last. This is bad practice.

At first the instructor will select the combinations you need to practise. These will begin simply, containing just two or three techniques. But as you become more proficient, so additional and more difficult techniques will be added. Eventually, you will be in a position to devise your own combination techniques, practising them in front of a mirror so that you see any mistakes or openings.

The following are examples of combination techniques, but do experiment and discover those which suit you best.

Front kick/ reverse punch

This is one of the simplest mixed combinations. As its name implies, it consists of a front kick followed by a reverse punch. Both techniques are aimed at the mid section.

Begin from left fighting stance by changing your guard and swivelling outwards on the left foot. Front kick with your right leg, then retrieve and set it down in a forward position. As your weight descends, draw back your right arm, twist the hips forwards and reverse punch strongly with your left fist. Withdraw the spent reverse punch afterwards, and bring the right fist into forward guard position. Front kick swivels the hips away from forward-facing, and so cocks reverse punch.

Front kick/roundhouse kick/reverse punch

This combination consists of two kicks and a punch, all performed to the mid section. Change your guard, swivel outwards on your leading foot and perform front kick. Retrieve the spent kick and set the foot down in a forward position. Twist the new lead foot outwards and bring your rear knee up and around, so as to close your body off from a counter-attack. Perform roundhouse kick to the mid section. Retrieve the kick and set your foot down in a forward position, landing lightly on the ball of your foot. Then engage your hips and perform a powerful reverse punch.

As in the previous case, the spent roundhouse kick lands with the punching hip pulled back and ready for immediate engagement by the reverse punch.

Roundhouse kick to head/back kick to mid section/reverse punch to mid section

This is a more complicated combination. Begin by rotating your shoulders in the direction of the roundhouse kick, then lift your rear foot and bring your kicking knee across your body. Be sure to raise your knee high, so that it points to the side of the opponent's face. Perform the kick, afterwards retrieving the foot and setting it down in a forward position with the hips still turned away from forward-facing.

Transfer your body weight on to the front foot and twist around on it, so that your back turns towards the opponent. Turn your head sharply to keep him in sight, then perform a back kick to the mid section. Set the spent kicking foot down in a forward position with the hips still turned away from the opponent. Then draw back your leading fist strongly, and twist your hips forcefully towards the front. Use this combined action to power the reverse punch. Withdraw the spent reverse punch, and resume an effective fighting stance.

The roundhouse kick causes the whole body to turn; the back kick is simply an extension of that motion. The turn out from the back kick continues the movement and, at the same time, it cocks the punching hip and prepares it for the last technique in the combination.

Pre-arranged sparring

Pre-arranged sparring follows on naturally from combination techniques, allowing karate skills to be tested on an opponent in controlled circumstances. No amount of training against pads or bags can equip you for combat with another person, so pre-arranged sparring is the ideal safe introduction.

There are various forms of pre-arranged sparring, but all have one common characteristic: both attacker and defender agree beforehand exactly what they are going to do, and who is going to do it. Under these circumstances, you might wonder what the value of pre-arranged sparring is. It teaches you how to time your response to an attack, and how to set up your distance and body position.

Not all pre-arranged sparring scenarios are realistic in the sense that you might expect to see them used on the street. This is because they are intended to train you in the *safe* use of certain basic blocks, movements and counters.

The most basic form of pre-arranged sparring consists of three identical attacks, each one following the other. Retreat from the first two, and make a counter on the third. Three-step routines are very useful for teaching timing and distance.

Look again at some of the blocking techniques practised earlier, and see how you might incorporate them into a three-step routine.

One-step sparring consists of a single agreed attack, and an immediate block and response to it. One-step routines are generally more realistic, and provide practice in making effective and practical responses to various forms of powerful attack.

The most realistic of all pre-arranged routines is semi-free sparring. This designates the attack but leaves the response free. The attacker may be restricted to using only roundhouse kick, for example, though he can change legs, kick high or low, and choose whether or not to use a step. The defender may use any technique in response.

All these various forms of pre-arranged sparring rely on certain protocols between the training partners. First of all, both partners must know which techniques are to be used, and who will use them. Secondly, attacks must always be made on target, otherwise the defender will become skilled at coping with inaccurate techniques. Thirdly, the speed of attack must be such that the defender can barely cope. Begin slowly and build up speed as the defender's skill level rises to meet the challenge. Going in too hard and too fast from the outset will intimidate your partner. Control your impacts to reduce the risk of injury, and always withdraw to a safe distance once you have performed your counters.

When you are proficient in dealing with this form of training, then you are ready for free sparring.

Free sparring

As a novice, you won't come across either **free sparring (jiu kumite)** or competition in a well-run club because both involve the exchange of blows and kicks of quite considerable force. Before you can spar you must be able to perform the basic techniques, devise combinations, and have a working knowledge of evasion, distance, timing and blocking. It is foolish to attempt free sparring before you have these skills.

Not all students like sparring, yet it is a necessary part of training. Those who are frightened can be encouraged by being placed with high grade students, who can be relied on to act sensibly. Others feel inadequate because their partner is obviously so much more proficient. These can be encouraged by always being partnered with students who will spar at their own pace, and teach them what to do.

Sometimes the instructor will make you spar at reduced speed. This is a valuable way of introducing novices to free sparring.

Sparring usually takes place at the end of the training session. You may select a partner, or the club instructor will select one for you. When selecting your own partner, find one of equal size and of either the same or a higher grade. Lower grades are less experienced at sparring, and have little control over their techniques. Novice karateka should not be allowed to spar together for this reason.

Large people develop considerable power, even when attacking slowly. Smaller opponents should be careful not to pit their strength directly against superior force. Take extra care when sparring with a lighter opponent.

You may not attack the opponent's shin, ankle, knee or groin. Close your hands fully when attacking the face, and control your impacts so that no injury is caused. Many facial injuries are caused when an opponent runs on to or ducks into a technique, so be especially careful. Use control also when attacking body targets.

Fist mitts cover the knuckles with a centimetre of foam, and reduce the likelihood of cutting the opponent's face through inadvertent contact. Choose mitts which leave the thumb free. Women should wear breast shields, and groin guards are essential for men. Shin guards or shin-instep protectors provide protection from bruises and grazes.

The object of free sparring is not to clobber your opponent, but to engage him in a trial of skill. It is sufficient merely to touch the opponent with your technique to indicate its success. If you are lightly tapped with a successful technique, withdraw for an instant before resuming. This signifies to the opponent that you recognise the attack is valid, and it prevents free sparring from degenerating into a brawl.

If ever free sparring gets out of hand, and/or your opponent seems to be getting over-excited, withdraw and bow. Then go and sit down cross-legged at the side of the dojo.

Kata

Kata is an advanced form of training which used to be the highest expression of karate before the advent of free sparring. The word *kata* does not translate readily; the approximation most often encountered is 'pattern' or 'form'.

Over 70 katas are practised currently, each consisting of a whole series of combination techniques arranged in a set order and direction. Katas are training drills which teach basic principles of technique application, focus, endurance, speed and balance. They also provide practice in linking combinations into a practical series of moves.

Some instructors attempt to explain the meaning of all the moves in kata. This is not easy to do since many katas originally involved the use of covert weapons; without these weapons, some techniques now have no obvious meaning. In other cases no true application can be traced easily. Personal interpretations can and are made of the various moves, in order to help the student's visualisation.

Most katas are symmetrical, starting from and finishing on the same spot. This fact is used by the instructor to check the uniformity of your performance.

You will come into contact with katas at an early stage in your training. The first katas you will learn are called **pinans**, or **heians**, depending on which school you join. The five pinans/heians were developed at the turn of the century as part of a special syllabus taught in schools. One must be learned for each of the elementary coloured belt grades.

The pinans/heians are followed by a whole series of more advanced katas, their number varying according to the style practised. Goju ryu has the least number of katas in its syllabus, Shito ryu the most.

At first the kata is practised in single steps, each performed at the instructor's command. Once you have learnt the moves, the instructor will have you perform them in sequences. Each sequence consists of a series of techniques separated by pauses, and represents a response to an imaginary sparring situation. During the pause, the next threat is being assessed.

Once you have learnt the techniques and the sequences in which they occur, you will be allowed to perform the kata all the way through. Remember that it is not a race.

At the conclusion of the kata the instructor will call **'Yamei!'** ('Stop!'), and you will withdraw from the last position into ready stance. At the end of kata practice, draw your heels together and perform a standing bow.

Don't blur techniques together. This is a common fault which shows itself when you perform the kata quicker than your skill level allows. Whenever you come to a pause, allow a count of at least two seconds to elapse before beginning the next sequence. Always turn your head to look before turning in a new direction.

Aim for fluidity and balance, and avoid unnecessary hesitations in performance. Breathe properly and concentrate your attention in the correct direction.

At certain points in the kata all of the body's mental and physical energies will be focused towards a block or a punch. When this happens, make a strong kiai (*see* page 14).

After many hours of practice the moves themselves will become automatic and your mind will be freed to dwell on the meaning of the kata itself. You can then concentrate on the visualisation, and so achieve a very skilled and meaningful performance.

Competition

Competition is a form of free sparring in which half or full point scores are awarded for successful techniques delivered to scoring areas. A maximum of three points may be scored by one opponent in a two or a three minute bout. The scoring areas include the head, the face and the body (excluding the groin and the tips of the shoulders). No contact to the throat or the groin is allowed, and no open-hand technique may be made to the face.

To score, the technique must have all the attributes of skill, and it must land in a controlled manner on the scoring area. Any infringement of the rules is dealt with by a warning, a half point penalty, a full point penalty or disqualification. In extreme cases, the offender can be disqualified from further participation in the tournament.

The match is controlled by a referee and a judge, who take positions on opposite sides of the competitors. An arbitrator sits at the edge of the match area to ensure that the rules are followed correctly by all parties. The match area itself is a mat 8 m square. Under no circumstances should competition ever take place on a concrete or stone floor.

Matches are fought in both team and individual categories. Men's teams consist of five men plus two reserves. Women's teams comprise three women plus one reserve. In the men's individual division, there is a cadet category for those aged over 16 and under 18, a junior category for those aged 18 to 21, and a senior category for those aged over 21. Women's individual competition is held in three weight divisions, senior men's competition in seven.

Tournaments also include team and individual kata competitions. These are typically held over three rounds, with the first round eliminating competitors

▲ *Competition karate*

down to 16 and the second round down to eight. The winner and the runners-up are selected from the last eight in the third round.

45

Glossary

Term	Pronunciation	Translation
chudan	chew-dan	mid section
chudan soto uke	chew-dan soe-toe-keh	mid section outer forearm block
chudan uchi uke	chew-dan oochy-keh	mid section inner forearm block
dojo	doe-joe	place of training in karatedo
empi	empee	elbow
fudodachi	foodoe-datchee	ready stance
gedan	gay-dan	lower section
gedan barai	gay-dan bar-eye	lower parry
Goju kai	go-joo kigh	hard/soft association
Goju ryu	go-joo ree-oo	hard/soft tradition (or style)
gyakuzuki	gee-ack-skee	reverse punch
heians	hay-ans	elementary katas
jiu dachi	joo-datchee	free fighting stance
jiu kumite	joo-koomittay	free fighting
jodan	joe-dan	upper body and head
jodan uke	joe-dan keh	head block
junzuki	jun-skee	lunge punch
karate	kah-ray-tay	empty hand

Term	Pronunciation	Translation
karatedo	kah-rah-tay-doe	way (or method) of karate
karategi	kah-rah-tay-gee	karate uniform
karateka	kah-rah-tay-kah	karate practitioner
kata	kah-tah	pattern or form
kiai	kee-eye	concentration of mental and physical energy
kime	kee-may	focus of impact energy
kiritsu	kirrits	stand up
kohei	koe-high	junior class-mate
kokutsudachi	koe-kuts-uh-datchee	back stance
kyokushinkai	kee-ock-oo-shin-kigh	way of ultimate truth association
maegeri	my-gerree	front kick
makiwara	makkee-warrah	punching post
mawashigeri	mah-wash-igg-eree	roundhouse kick
mawatte	mah-wattay	turn
oizuki	oy-skee	another name for lunge punch
Okinawa-te	oe-kin-ah-wa tay	karate's Okina-wan predecessor

Term	Pronunciation	Translation
otagai ni rei	oh-tag-eye nee-ray	bow to class-mates
pinans	pee-nans	another name for the five elementary katas
Ryukyu kempo	reeyoo-keeyoo kem-poe	Okinawan boxing (or 'fist-way')
sanchin	san-chin	name of stance and kata favoured in Goju ryu
sempai	sem-pie	senior class-mate
sensei	sen-say	teacher
sensei ni rei	sen-say nee ray	bow to the teacher
shikodachi	shicko-datchee	straddle (or horse-riding) stance
Shito kai	sh'toe kigh	Shito association
Shito ryu	sh'toe ree-yoo	Shito tradition (or style)
shotei	show-tay	palm heel
Shoto	show-toe	Gichin Funakoshi's pen-name
Shotokai	show-toe kigh	Shoto's association
Shotokan	show-toe can	Shoto's club

Term	Pronunciation	Translation
shukokai	shoo-koe-kigh	way for all association
shuto	sh'toe	knife hand
shuto uke	sh'toe keh	knife hand block
suki uke	s'kee keh	scooping block
surikomi	soo-rih-koe-mee	one step
Tani ha Shito ryu	tarnee-hah-sh'toe-ree-yoo	Chojiro Tani's style of Shito karate
tettsui	tet-swee	hammer fist
to-te	toe-tay	another name for karate's Okinawan predecessor
uraken	oo-rah-ken	back fist
ushiro geri	oo-shirroe-gerree	back kick
Wado kai	wah-doe kigh	way of peace association
Wado ryu	wah-doe ree-yoo	way of peace tradition (or style)
yamei	yam-may	stop
yoko geri	yoe-koe gerree	side kick
zenkutsu dachi	zen-kut-soo datchee	forward stance

Index